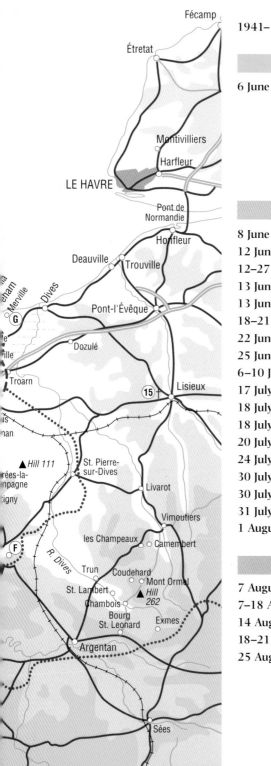

N

| 0 | 10 | 20 Km |
| 0 | 5 | 10 Miles |

D-DAY AND THE
BATTLE OF NORMANDY 1944

Preparations for Invasion

Soon after the almost miraculous evacuation of the British Expeditionary Force from Dunkirk in 1940, leaving France and Northern Europe in German hands, Winston Churchill set up the Combined Operations Staff to undertake the preparation for the invasion of Europe. This was to be, four years later, an undertaking without precedent for complexity and co-ordination in the history of warfare, and essential in defeating Hitler.

On the mainland of Europe, Hitler was turning his attention to ensuring the defence of the territory he had seized and in March 1942 recalled Field Marshal von Rundstedt from retirement to take command. The failure of the Allies' practical experiment in landing on the enemy coast, the raid on Dieppe the following August, reassured the Germans, wrongly, that massive coastal defences were the answer to invasion. They pressed ahead with the building of the Atlantic Wall, a series of mighty concrete batteries and beach obstacles that was intended to stretch from the Low Countries to Brittany.

The sacrifices made by the Canadian forces at Dieppe – fewer than a third of them returned to England – were not in vain, for vital lessons were learned by the Allies. The ability to ship supplies – food, munitions, equipment and reinforcements – to the invaders was crucial, but frontal attack on a suitable port like Dieppe was clearly suicide. From this grew the determination to 'take the port with us' – to build artificial harbours, and to by-pass fixed defensive installations.

The selection of the invasion site was fundamental to success, and the Pas de Calais was obviously attractive, with a narrow sea crossing, direct access to the heartland of Germany and close to airfields in England. Here the Germans created the most formidable defences, and here the Allies' Operation FORTITUDE deceived the Germans into thinking a huge army stood ready in south-east England and kept half the German forces awaiting the 'real' invasion for weeks after D-Day.

BELOW: American forces ready for France. The equipment stockpiled in south and south-west England was real, while dummy tanks and trucks in the south-east helped to create the illusion of plans to invade the Pas de Calais. (IWM)

TOP RIGHT: From the Overlord Embroidery in the D-Day Museum, Portsmouth, King George VI with, left to right, General Eisenhower, Commander-in-Chief 21st Army Group General Sir Bernard L. Montgomery, Chief of the Imperial General Staff Field Marshal Sir Alan Brooke and Prime Minister Winston S. Churchill. The scene recalls two visits to Normandy, the King's on 16 June and Churchill and Brooke's on 12 June. (D-Day Museum)

RIGHT: The Supreme Allied Commander, General Dwight D. Eisenhower. (NA)

BELOW: Field Marshal Erwin Rommel (right), commander of the fighting forces the Allies were to face, Army Group B, with the Commander-in-Chief West, Field Marshal Gerd von Rundstedt (left). Successive commanders were hamstrung by Hitler's mistrust and interference. (B)

The planners gathered all possible information on the true target, the Normandy beaches between Caen and the Cotentin peninsula, as well as the false destination. Air photography, clandestine landings and data from the French Resistance contributed. Special equipment was developed for the landings. All over England the forces gathered under the Supreme Allied Commander General Dwight D. Eisenhower: 20 American divisions, 14 British, three Canadian and one each from Poland and France, with nearly 8,000 aircraft, over 4,000 landing craft and ships and nearly 300 fighting vessels; 2,876,439 men in total.

Army Commander-in-Chief General Sir Bernard Montgomery's plan for Operation OVERLORD was to secure the eastern flank along the Orne, including Caen and Falaise, in the first three weeks of the campaign with British, Canadian, French and Polish troops. Meanwhile, in the west, the American forces of Lt General Omar Bradley would take the Cotentin peninsula, freeing Cherbourg to act as a supply harbour, then thrust south to the Loire to create a north-south front, before the whole force rolled eastwards towards Paris and the Seine.

That events turned out differently is no surprise; the Germans could hardly be expected to co-operate with the Allies' plans! The German defence, under Field Marshal Erwin Rommel, dominated by Hitler's unreal policy of yielding nothing, led to a war of attrition that reminded commanders of the fearful battles of the First World War. And always present in Montgomery's mind was the knowledge that Britain had no further reserves of manpower to draw on.

American Airborne Landings

ABOVE: Market day at Sainte-Mère-Eglise; a peaceful scene overshadowed by a reminder of the drama that marked the early hours of 6 June, 1944 – the effigy of an American paratrooper hangs from the church tower.

The little town of Sainte-Mère-Eglise stands on a ridge that carries the main road from Cherbourg down to Carentan, overlooking the salt-marshes behind the sand dunes facing the sea to the east and the valley of the river Merderet, a tributary of the Douve, to the west. The marshes and the river valleys had been flooded by the Germans, so this ridge and the causeways across the marshes had to be secured to enable the troops approaching Utah Beach to come ashore and move inland. Soon after 1.30 a.m. on 6 June the men of the American 82nd and 101st Divisions began their landings.

The aeroplanes and gliders swept over the land through thick cloud from the direction of the Channel Islands, heading east. Their formations were harassed by flak, anti-aircraft fire, which, combined with poor navigation and the fear of overshooting the landing zone and dropping troops in the sea, led to a widely scattered drop. Many lost their lives without firing a shot, drowned in the floods and marshes.

The 82nd's 505 Parachute Infantry Regiment dropped not only close to Sainte-Mère-Eglise, but some of them right into the village square where the citizens were passing buckets from the town pump to douse a fire. Many men were shot as they descended, and John Steele found himself dangling from the church tower shamming death to save his life. His comrades had landed safely close by to the west, and entered the village quietly, taking the Germans by surprise and liberating it by 4.30 a.m.

Elsewhere the scattered troops gathered themselves together, clicking little metal toy crickets as recognition signals in the darkness. They formed themselves into impromptu units and attacked the enemy; surprise was almost complete.

To the south, and closer to the beaches, near Sainte-Marie-du-Mont the drop was even more widely scattered. General Maxwell Taylor found himself entirely alone and it was some time before he made contact with sufficient of the 101st to start operations to secure the causeways leading from the beaches. In spite of the inaccuracy of the drop, the job was done.

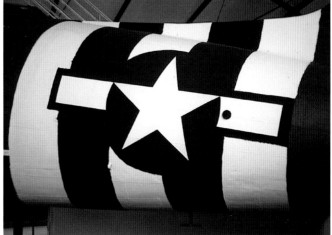

LEFT: A detail from one of the commemorative windows in the church.

RIGHT: The broad white bands added to the conventional identification markings on the fuselage of the aircraft used to tow invading gliders were designed to aid recognition by Allied fighters. This aeroplane forms part of the magnificent display in the Airborne Museum at Sainte-Mère-Eglise.

'Hobart's Funnies'

A major factor in the D-Day landings was the use of specially modified tanks – widely known as 'Hobart's Funnies' after the man under whose control they had been built, Major General Sir Percy Hobart. These included 'Crabs' equipped with flails to explode mines, 'Crocodiles' acting as mobile flame-throwers, 'Petards' with a 290mm mortar to fire a 40lb (18kg) projectile for destroying fortifications and AVREs, Armoured Vehicle Royal Engineers, with various devices such as bridge-laying equipment or huge bundles of wood to fill in tank traps (see page 15). Perhaps most surprising of all were the 'D-Ds' – the Duplex Drive M4 Sherman tanks. They were fitted with propellers and capable of amphibious operation. A canvas skirt was fixed to the tank and 36 inflatable tubes raised it up to be secured with a metal frame.

The large illustration shows D-Ds in a pre D-Day exercise in England. One tank is entirely hidden within its canvas hull while others have lowered theirs. In the small picture a D-D is entering the water from a landing craft. It is obvious that, by the time it reaches the end of the ramp, even a slight sea will start to swamp it. The rough weather of early June led to the sinking of numerous D-Ds in the landings, and serious loss of life.

(Pictures courtesy The Tank Museum)

Utah Beach and Pointe du Hoc

RIGHT: American troops landing at Utah Beach. German resistance was slight and soon overcome, and the sea was calm. This gentle beginning was to be followed by fighting that tested the GIs to the utmost. (TM)

ABOVE: The roads beyond the beach now commemorate the names of those who gave their lives to liberate this land.

OPPOSITE, TOP: The ruins of a defensive blockhouse stand on the dunes close by the intended landing place on Utah Beach; the main force reached shore further south. Inland the dunes give way to wet, marshy pasture, intersected with drainage ditches and crossed by just a few causeways. The airborne troops succeeded in securing these, as planned, to get the invaders off the beach.

The weather in the Channel in the first week of June 1944 was so bad that the German Headquarters was convinced that invasion was impossible. Indeed, it had been delayed a full 24 hours before Eisenhower gave the command to attack, but just before dawn on 6 June the German soldiers defending Utah Beach were galvanised into the alert by the massive bombardment unleashed upon them by the battleships accompanying the invading force. The landing craft, sheltered here by the land from the heavy seas, had already been on the water for over two hours, creeping the 11 miles (18km) towards their objective. The mass of vessels staggered the defenders, while the lack of serious reply from the shore cheered the nervous troops in the landing craft, most of whom were going into action for the first time. They were on the look-out for the Luftwaffe; dive-bombers were expected, but the skies were clear. Here, as elsewhere, the Germans did little or nothing to dispute Allied command of the air.

As they drew nearer to the beach it became clear to Brigadier General Theodore Roosevelt Jr that the tide was sweeping them south of their intended landing point. He decided to press on, and was rewarded by the lucky chance that this part of the beach was much more lightly defended than the planned landing place. The Americans were swiftly ashore, soon to be joined by their amphibious tanks and pushing inland. Meanwhile the heavy German guns of the Crisbecq battery concerned themselves in duelling with the navy. By the end of the day more than 23,000 men had come ashore with only some 200 casualties.

To the east, threatening both Utah Beach and Omaha Beach, and capable of shelling the invasion fleet as well, stood the six-gun battery at Pointe du Hoc. The task of removing this danger was given to the American 2nd Ranger Battalion under the command of Lt Col James E. Rudder. Pointe du Hoc is one of two prominent sets of cliffs jutting out to sea west of Omaha Beach. It was towards the other, Pointe de la Percée, that Rudder found himself heading through the spray and half-light of that June dawn.

Altering course and landing as best they could from their virtually swamped craft, three of which had already sunk, the Rangers found themselves about 500 yards (450m) east of their intended landing point. The attempt to use ladders mounted on amphibious trucks (DUKWs) failed because of the shell craters on the beach, while the grapnels they hoped to fire up

the cliffs were dragged back by the sodden ropes. The cliff had to be climbed, in the face of enemy fire and the hand grenades that were rolled down on the attackers. A bomber raid drove the Germans under cover, and fire from the warships out to sea kept them there, allowing the Rangers to scale the cliff and overrun the position. There were no guns in the emplacements.

Rudder moved his men swiftly inland in search of the missing weapons, and found them concealed in an orchard close to the main coastal road where they were destroyed. By this time he had lost perhaps 15 per cent of the 225 men who landed,

ABOVE: The German Cemetery at La Cambe.

RIGHT: On the cliff-top at Pointe du Hoc an austere memorial to the Rangers stands above a calm sea, mounted on one of the emplacements they gave so much to conquer.

but the greatest test was still to come. German counter-attacks drove them back to a line only 200 yards (180m) from the cliffs, and they suffered from their own supporting bomber and naval artillery fire as well.

It was not until midday two days later, on 8 June, that they were relieved by troops fighting through from Omaha Beach, by which time 60 per cent of the Rangers had become casualties.

Omaha Beach

It would be hard to imagine a greater contrast, short of outright failure, to the experience of the troops landing at Utah Beach than that of their comrades at Omaha. Here, further east, the Cotentin peninsula offered no shelter from the heavy seas and here the forces the invaders faced were of a different calibre. Unknown to the Allies, the 716th Coastal Defence Division was not alone in guarding this part of the coast. The 352nd Infantry Division was present on exercise, doubling the forces available to the Germans. The coast itself was a formidable obstacle, sandy beaches fronting 100-feet (30m) cliffs through which only five small gullies or draws offered a way inland.

The first error made was to commence the landing run too far offshore, nearly 12 miles (19km) out instead of the seven (11km) the British decided on. The seas

ABOVE: 'The Spirit of American Youth' stands guard over the vast American cemetery at Saint-Laurent-sur-Mer above Omaha Beach.

RIGHT: Omaha Beach from a gun emplacement in the western cliffs. Landing craft and troops were at the mercy of a deadly fire from such positions. Below, the stranded caisson of the wrecked Mulberry harbour provides the landward foundation for a modern jetty.

overwhelmed many of the landing craft, and those that made it by 6.30 a.m. had been going for three hours by then. Of the 32 D-D tanks that started 6,000 yards (5,500m) from the shore, 27 sank. The engineers responsible for clearing obstacles were mostly blown way off-course. Artillery loaded onto DUKWs caused them to capsize and was lost. As the survivors of the first wave approached the beach, the only firing was from the Allied ships giving cover, but the second the ramps dropped the defenders opened up with deadly accuracy. Their bunkers had been built with the great bulk of their concrete facing the sea and the gun-ports looking along the four miles (6km) of beach, protected from shelling from the sea and perfectly arranged to enfilade the troops struggling through the waves and attempting to cross the 100 yards (90m) of sand. The effect on the brave but inexperienced Americans was terrible.

Into the turmoil of wrecked landing craft, burning vehicles and dead and wounded men the successive waves of invaders came to suffer similar loss. By noon most of the 1st and 29th Infantry were still pinned down on the beach, and the American 1st Army commander, Lt

General Omar Bradley, seriously considered evacuating them.

'Every man who set foot on Omaha Beach that day was a hero', Bradley said later. But it was the particular heroism of small groups and individuals that saved the day. A company of Rangers, originally intended for the reinforcement of the force at Pointe du Hoc, managed with great loss to gain the foot of the western cliffs and proceeded to knock out one bunker after another. Brigadier General Norman D. Cota of the 29th strode about, apparently charmed against enemy bullets, to rally his men. Colonel Taylor did likewise. Slowly the German positions were taken and the great weight of the American force made itself felt.

The early success of the German defenders faded. Ammunition ran low. Their reserves, the 915th Regiment, were on a wild-goose chase inland, seeking the paratroopers reported as having been dropped before dawn; in fact a drop of dummies. As evening approached the Americans had gained the cliffs and were streaming up the exits from the beach to secure a bridgehead no more than a mile deep, but a bridgehead it was, at a cost of over 2,000 casualties.

ABOVE LEFT: American photographer Robert Capa landed with the troops under heavy fire early on 6 June to record their struggle to survive in the heavy seas and amongst obstacles that offered trivial shelter. (Magnum)

LEFT: From their trenches on the cliff-top the defenders dominated the beach. (IWM)

The eastern, or left, flank of the Allied landing beaches, Sword, was on the River Orne which flows through Caen ten miles (16km) on to the sea at Ouistreham. Alongside the river is the Orne Canal, capable of carrying sea-going vessels, and to the east of this valley a ridge separates it from the valley of the Dives. The Germans had flooded the Dives and thus, provided the British could secure the ridge and blow the bridges over the floods, created a moat that would protect the invaders from counterattack from the east. To support their airborne forces, the Allies had to capture the Orne bridges undamaged.

The lifting bridge over the canal at Benouville, and its companion over the river, were defended and it was essential that a surprise attack should be made. The glider-borne men of the Oxfordshire and Buckinghamshire Light Infantry were chosen for this task, under the command of Major John Howard. Just before 11.00 p.m. on 5 June they took off from England, to be released about an hour later for the glide in to the objective. The leading glider bounced and smashed its way to a halt, exactly where planned, only 50 yards (45m) from the canal bridge, its two companions close behind. Howard relates his first sensation was that everything had gone dark. Had he been blinded? To his relief he realised that his helmet had been driven down over his eyes. Raising it he looked at his watch. It had stopped at 16 minutes past midnight.

To the joy of the Gondrée family in the café beyond the canal, the men of the Ox & Bucks took the bridge in a swift fight and within minutes D-Day's first objectives,

ABOVE: The memorial to the defenders of Les Bois des Monts and Château St Côme. Reduced to only 85 men, the 9th Parachute Battalion were ordered here on 7 June to hold out at all costs against a German counterattack. More men from other units swelled their numbers to 270, but they were still outnumbered by four to one. They held.

RIGHT: April 1944. Glider troops on exercise. (IWM)

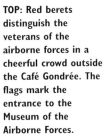

TOP: Red berets distinguish the veterans of the airborne forces in a cheerful crowd outside the Café Gondrée. The flags mark the entrance to the Museum of the Airborne Forces.

LEFT: 8 June 1944. Two of Major Howard's gliders on the banks of the Caen Canal at Pegasus Bridge. (IWM)

what became known as Pegasus Bridge and the river bridge, the target of another group of glider troops, were in British hands.

At Merville, on the northern tip of the ridge, Allied reconnaissance had observed

LEFT: The river Dives, near Troarn, flows slowly across marshy fields that were flooded by the Germans. The bridge close by was blown by Major J. C. A. Roseveare and a party of one officer and seven Engineers, who made an audacious dash by jeep through the town to reach the target and create a moat to protect the eastern flank.

LEFT: June 1993. Close by the marker where he landed in the first glider, Wally Parr points out how Pegasus Bridge was taken, while his comrade, the bearded Charlie Gardner, savours his first visit since June 1944.

the construction of a large battery with, it was believed, four 150mm guns able to shell Sword beach. The battery was surrounded with two concentric barbed wire entanglements with a minefield between them. The task of putting it out of action was given to the 9th Parachute Battalion under Lt Col Terence Otway, and the job had to be completed after a bombing raid at 3.00 a.m. and before HMS *Arethusa*, should she get no success signal, started shelling at 5.30 a.m. A total of 550 men were to parachute in and three gliders with 60 more men were to land within the perimeter as the attack took place. In the event, Otway found himself with only 150 men, no special mine-detecting equipment, no anti-tank guns, no engineers, signallers, medics or mortars and only one machine-gun. The one glider that arrived, lacking a landing signal, overflew.

Using bomb craters to avoid mines and enlarging gaps in the wire with Bangalore torpedoes they pressed forward, and at the fearful price of losing nearly half the men, the objective was gained on time. The guns found were old Czech howitzers.

German counter-attacks in strength were slow in coming. Not only was the invasion unexpected, and Rommel absent at home, but a fatal division of command meant the armoured Panzer divisions could only be deployed on orders from Berlin. The hard-pressed Airborne troops were soon reinforced by Lord Lovat's 6th Commando, Kieffer's 1st French Commando and other regiments disentangled from the traffic jams of Sword beach. With the eastern flank thus established, operations towards Caen could proceed.

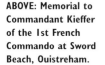

ABOVE: Memorial to Commandant Kieffer of the 1st French Commando at Sword Beach, Ouistreham.

Through the night of 5/6 June RAF bombers raided the coastal defences, and as dawn broke the USAF took over, while the escort warships of the approaching invasion fleet added their salvos to the onslaught. At 7.25 a.m., precisely on time, the first tanks gained Sword Beach and started their clearance operations. The special modifications made to the tanks, Hobart's Funnies, could now show their worth. The flails of the Crabs cleared minefields, Crocodiles spewed fire from their flamethrowers and both regular guns and the heavy weapons of the Petards struck at concrete defensive emplacements.

Though not without cost in men and machines, the landings were achieved very much as planned, but as the day went on the tide rose higher than anticipated, the storms of the last few days piling the Atlantic into the Channel. The beach was reduced from an expected 30 yards (27m) wide to a mere 30 feet (9m), the landing craft pushed inexorably shorewards and a serious traffic jam developed, preventing armour and infantry moving swiftly inland as required. Meanwhile the sluggish German response was giving way to action; the Panzers were on their way.

Inland, about a mile (1.6km) from the beach itself, rises a long ridge which turns south to form the side of the valley of the Orne while, to the west, it continues to overlook the river Seulles behind Juno

Beach. Though of no great height, it gives commanding views across the landing ground and was the site of a radar station within substantial fortifications at Douvres as well as Morris and Hillman forts to the east, near Colleville. It was along the route dominated by Hillman, in fact the German coastal forces headquarters, that the main thrust to Caen was to go. The Suffolk Regiment, unsupported by naval artillery, as the liaison officer had been killed, and only getting tank support in the afternoon, eventually overcame the obstacle bunker by bunker.

The dash for Caen failed. The 2nd Battalion, The King's Shropshire Light

Infantry, did more than could possibly be expected, but lacking the full artillery and tank support they needed, they were stopped at Lebisey, the village on a hill overlooking Caen and only three miles (4km) from the city centre. By the end of the day the British were well established ashore, but still separated from their Canadian Allies to the west by a gap now filled by 21st Panzer and with numerous pockets of enemy troops still showing determined resistance in the sector.

On Juno Beach the Canadians found the height of the tide a mixed blessing. There were shoals offshore to hinder the approach, but these were swiftly covered by the advancing waters, sweeping the landing craft in more quickly than planned. The infantry arrived ahead of the armour, and the manoeuvering craft ran

foul of each other and of the Hedgehogs. The Hedgehogs were pyramids of steel struts with mines fixed on top, and were built on all the beaches to deter and destroy invaders. When exposed they could be avoided and neutralised, but submerged, they were a deadly peril. The D-Ds did well at the more sheltered western end of the beach and were able to support the infantry in the street fighting of the coastal towns.

Luc-sur-Mer marked the border between Sword and Juno, and the 21st Panzer penetrated this far in their counter-attack, to find their comrades still in place, but the arrival of 46th Royal Marine Commando the following morning put an end to any German plan to reinforce their hold on the gap between the Canadians and the British.

At Bernières rough sea prevented use of the D-Ds, and the Queen's Own Rifles of Canada suffered fearfully against the substantial complex of bunkers. A flak ship moved in, almost aground, to give supporting fire, and the defences were overcome. The Regiment de la Chaudière were next ashore, but were held up inland and successive waves of landing craft contributed to another great pile-up of men and machines. The beach was not working efficiently as a landing area until mid-afternoon, starving the advancing forces of the support they needed.

The aim of the 9th Brigade, following up and then passing through the landing forces, was to push on south and east to Carpiquet airfield, just south-west of Caen. They came within four miles (6km) of the city that day, but in insufficient strength to resist the German counter-attacks. It was not until 9 July, five weeks later, that the airfield was finally taken.

14   Gold Beach and the Mulberry Harbour

The westernmost of the British beaches, Gold Beach, flanked Juno at La Rivière and stretched west to Le Hamel, under the cliffs topped by St Côme, beyond which, in the first inlet, is Arromanches and further on is the narrow gap in the cliffs that shelters Port-en-Bessin, the start of the American sector. Between the two, on the clifftop, stood the four-gun Le Chaos battery near Longues with its surrounding anti-aircraft guns, searchlights and observation bunker.

men while under fire. Following were the 151st Brigade with orders to make for Bayeux. By evening they were on the outskirts of the town, and in full occupation a day later. On 14 June Bayeux became the scene for the first executive act of the provisional French government, the appointment of M Raymond Triboulet as Sous-Préfet by General de Gaulle.

At Arromanches the Allies established one of the two Mulberry Harbours.

BELOW: The Mulberry harbour at Arromanches full of shipping in 1944 (IWM) and, at the foot of the page, the coast today. The remains of caissons and pontoons may still be seen.

This threat was swiftly silenced by fire from HMS *Ajax* at dawn, and a gun brought back into action that afternoon was dealt with by the French cruiser *Georges Leygues*.

The effect of adverse weather here on D-Day was possibly the most severe of all. It was decided to carry the armour all the way in on landing craft rather than risk a launch of D-Ds into the rough water. The beach was backed by low and marshy land, and here Hobart's Funnies were at their most effective, clearing mines and bridging ditches to speed the advance.

At La Rivière the landings went relatively smoothly and the Green Howards were mainly challenged by the battery at Mont Fleury. It was during the action to destroy this defence work and move inland that CSM Stan Hollis won the only VC awarded for valour on D-Day itself. Single-handed, he took two German pill-boxes and later in the day rescued two of his

TOP RIGHT:
Headstones in the British cemetery at Ryes testify to the sacrifice of men of the Merchant Navy and of the RAF.

BELOW: The massive 155mm naval guns of the battery at Longues-sur-Mer.

CENTRE RIGHT:
Some of 'Hobart's Funnies' – two Sherman Crabs with their mine-bursting flails and a Churchill AVRE bridge-laying tank. (TM)

BELOW RIGHT: A floating pier at Arromanches. (IWM)

Gooseberries, cement-filled block ships, were used on all beaches as breakwaters, but the Mulberry was a full-blown port, with caissons, great concrete boxes, sunk inside the ring of Gooseberries to form a solid wall and floating piers and roadways allowing unloading of ships at all states of the tide. Construction of the prefabricated units was carried out in England, and the whole towed across the Channel. Assembly started on 9 June, and by 18 June a great arc of caissons was in place. The next day a storm commenced and blew for three days from the north-east, turning the whole coast into a lee shore, fatal to ships at anchor. The Mulberry at Omaha was entirely wrecked, and the Arromanches harbour severely damaged, delaying the arrival of vital supplies. The installation was originally designed to endure for 100 days; its remains survive today.

LEFT: The characteristic form of the Comité du Débarquement Signal Monument records General de Gaulle's speech to the liberated French at Isigny on 14 June 1944.

to defending the bridgehead from any further attack from the south (there was none) and pushing west and north for Cherbourg.

The 4th US Infantry had already started north from Utah Beach. These were green, inexperienced troops and they suffered in consequence. Although supported by air strikes, including the use of napalm, they sustained 2,200 casualties in a week. The river valleys to the west were either flooded or boggy. Tanks could not be deployed and had to stick to the roads, while the 'bocage', the patchwork of little fields, made perfect terrain for defensive operations, which the Germans exploited with lethal skill. The bulk of German striking power was tied up in the defence of Caen, and only 2nd Panzer could be spared to move up from Caumont into the peninsula.

The bocage was crushingly discouraging country for the Allies. The ancient fields were divided by hedges and ditches, so old that they formed earth embankments waist- or even shoulder-high. Even where there were no marshes, tanks had difficulty in moving freely, so the infantry had to fight their way forward alone, hedge by hedge and field by field, unable to see the enemy and exposed to withering fire when they broke cover. Progress was slow and costly.

To prevent reinforcements reaching the

BELOW: The bocage, a countryside of hedges, woods, small fields and narrow roads, was skilfully exploited by the defending Germans.

After their fearful experience at Omaha Beach, the US 2nd Division had secured the bridgehead by noon the following day, made contact with their Allies to the east and started to move inland and towards their comrades in the west. La Cambe was taken that same day and the American forces closed in on Carentan amidst the floods and marshes of the Douves estuary. From the foot of the Cotentin peninsula the US 101st Airborne moved with the greater energy and skill that marked the performance of these crack troops. The two met and, on 14 June, having successfully resisted the counter-attack of the 17th SS Panzer Grenadiers, were able to turn their attention

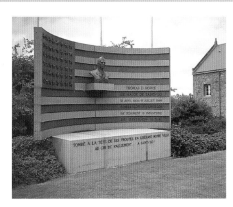

sea, the Allies controlled the air, and the Americans, with their superior numbers and material, were closing in on land. Nevertheless the Germans fought with amazing vigour and determination.

On 22 June waves of aircraft, some 1,000 in all, subjected the defenders to heavy bombing, and the artillery barrage was intense. The German lines slowly crumbled, and the advancing troops found themselves learning the skills of house-to-house fighting as they entered the town. Even after the surrender of von Schlieben himself on 26 June, resistance continued and it was not until 1 July that the Americans were in control. The port installations had been comprehensively demolished. It had been intended to bring in 150,000 tons of stores here by 25 July, but it was not until September that Cherbourg was capable of handling cargo at the required rate, by which time the need had already passed.

For the push south the target had been Coutances, but the painfully slow progress made in this tough terrain led Bradley to lower his sights to the seizure of St Lô and the road from that town to Périers. Mont-Castre, to the east of La Haye-du-Puits, was reached on 3 July. The attack started on the 7th and in the two days it took to advance some four miles (6km) 2,000 Americans became casualties. The approach to St Lô was equally agonizing. The Germans threw in the remains of Panzer Lehr, reduced to 66 from 190 operational tanks in the fighting against the British near Tilly, but they were held by the fighter bombers and artillery. After two weeks of solid fighting, St Lô became a symbol of the suffering of the GIs in the bocage. On the evening of 18 July the 116th Regiment entered the northern outskirts of the town while the 115th came in from the east, bearing with them the body of Major Howie to fulfil his oath to reach St Lô.

defenders of Cherbourg, Bradley thrust for the western coast, the 82nd Airborne taking Saint-Sauveur-le-Vicomte on 16 June and the 90th US Infantry securing Barneville-sur-Mer on the 18th, in readiness for any pressure from the south. The German commander, von Schlieben, regrouped his forces to offer resistance in depth from some eleven miles (18km) away to Cherbourg itself. However, he was cut off. No supplies could reach him by

LEFT: American troops
enter the shattered
ruins of St Gilles, near
St Lô. (Capa/Magnum)

All this had taken far longer and was at a much greater cost than Bradley had anticipated. The Americans were paying the price of having neglected the infantry in favour of forming crack outfits and special units. But soon, with German resources steadily draining away around Caen, their opportunity was to come.

FAR LEFT: Lt General
von Schlieben and
Rear Admiral
Hennecke, Sea Defence
Commander,
Normandy, emerge
from shelter to
surrender to the
Americans at
Cherbourg. (IWM)

The British Thrust to Villers-Bocage

TOP LEFT: The villagers of Tilly abandon their ruined homes. (IWM)

TOP RIGHT: The Château de Creullet, Montgomery's HQ.

ABOVE: In the tiny cemetery known as Jerusalem, near Chouain, to the north of Tilly, lies the body of Private Banks. He was 16 years old.

While forces advancing on Caen had been halted short of the city on D-Day, the progress towards Bayeux was comparatively unhindered and the town was occupied on 7 June. The 50th Division pushed on south towards Tilly-sur-Seulles, while Montgomery, in his headquarters set up near Creully on 8 June, was coming to the conclusion that head-on attacks for Caen were likely to be too costly. Detecting a gap in the German defences, an attack round the western flank towards Villers-Bocage and then on towards Falaise was planned.

The troops approaching Tilly found themselves up against Panzer Lehr, newly arrived from Chartres and, although mauled by the airforce on the way, formidable opponents. The German Panther tanks outgunned the tanks of the British, and carried heavier armour. Here they showed the power that was to slow Allied progress throughout the campaign. In the process the little village of Tilly was reduced to rubble.

Attempting to outflank the Germans, the 7th Armoured Division, the 'Desert Rats', swept around to the west as far as Villers-Bocage, only to meet another new arrival on the scene, 2nd Panzer with their yet more powerful Tiger tanks.

Pausing outside the village on the Caen road on the morning of 13 June, they were attacked by the greatest German tank ace of the war, Michael Wittmann. The two Tigers with him engaged the British while Wittmann himself roared down the road to Villers-Bocage, destroying much of the transport there and leaving the whole formation shattered. He then attacked the tanks in the village, accounting for another six before he was gone.

Communications with their forward troops having broken down, the British commanders assumed the Germans had plugged the gap and failed to reinforce their forward troops. Rommel was, in fact, struggling to put enough units into the sector to hold the line but wisely concentrated on the key locations. By 15 June the British had withdrawn and the opportunity to exploit holes in the defensive line had passed. Although the Germans were outnumbered they maintained a thin line of observation posts along the full length of the front line, moving reinforcements swiftly in response to Allied attacks. This form of defence could succeed for a time, while sufficient men survived, and while the German command remained in the skilled hands of Rommel.

South-west of Caen a wedge of higher, open terrain, with a superb vantage point over the surrounding country at Hill 112, is defined on the southern side by the valley of the River Orne and on the northern edge by the narrow cutting of the Odon, with more open country between it and Tilly. This was to be the scene of a battle of ferocious intensity during the last days of June.

A huge barrage by the army and navy on 25 June was followed by an advance reminiscent of the First World War against the stubborn defence of the Hitlerjugend. In unseasonable rain and mud, 15th Scottish Division led the attack, and on 26 June the Argyll and Sutherland Highlanders seized the bridge at Tourmauville, allowing the 11th Armoured Division to pour across to Hill 112 itself, only to be repulsed by the 1st SS Panzer. The bridge at Gavrus was also secured before the desperate counter-attack came in from the west. Fresh from the Eastern front, the SS 2nd Armoured Division joined 9th and 10th SS Panzer to threaten a line from Gavrus as far north as Cheux, but by 28 June they had to concede failure against a British resistance at least the equal of their own against the Allies further south.

The foothold south of the Odon was retained and became the scene of dogged fighting that lasted for more than a month – the battle for Hill 112. Here the 43rd Wessex Division was put under pressure in Operation Jupiter, on 10 July, to break through to the Orne. Once more the result was a failure.

The Duke of Cornwall's Light Infantry also suffered severely. They managed to dig in on Hill 112 but the attacks of the seemingly invulnerable Tiger tanks in support of SS Panzergrenadiers eventually drove them off. Early in August fighting was to move to areas further west and when, finally, British troops surveyed the German side of the hill, they saw a wilderness of shell holes and corpses.

ABOVE: 27 June; a Panther tank of the SS 2nd Armoured Division burns at Cheux. (IWM)

RIGHT: Near Hill 112, the monument to the 43rd Wessex Division.

FAR RIGHT: The Odon valley hid bridges essential to the advance.

Since the evening of D-Day, when the British found themselves within a few miles of the city, Caen had remained an elusive objective, stubbornly held by the Germans. The open country beyond beckoned, offering, it seemed, scope to release the armoured divisions to race away south and space to create bases for the airforce.

While the Odon shook under the impact of attack and counter-attack, the Canadians, the Regiment de la Chaudière and the Queen's Own Rifles, took the village of Carpiquet and spent the four days until 9 July clearing the airfield of fanatical resistance by the Hitlerjugend.

On 6 July an air-raid on Caen started a fire that raged for eleven days, and on the night of 8/9 July 2,500 tons of bombs were dropped on the city. The damage was immense. The shattered citizens took what shelter they could but some 3,000 did not survive. The homeless seeking cover in the ancient Abbaye aux Hommes were miraculously untouched. On the morning of 9 July Canadian forces entered from the west, while the British made their way in from the north, against continued defiance by the Luftwaffe 16th Division and the shambles created by the bombing. By early afternoon the Germans had yielded that part of the city north of the river but it was to be 18 July before the right bank was in Allied hands.

ABOVE: St-Etienne boasts an ancient link with England; the grave of William the Conqueror.

LEFT: The church of St-Etienne (St Stephen), Abbaye aux Hommes, survived the bombardment.

ABOVE: A British soldier waits his chance to fire on a German sniper in the ruins of the town. (IWM)

ABOVE RIGHT: Commandos advance on Caen through the woods and hedges to the north of the town. (IWM)

LEFT: The houses near the Abbaye aux Hommes still bear the scars of war.

RIGHT: Damage to the old town centre was fearful and French civilian casualties ran to thousands. (IWM)

More than a month had passed since the Allies had poured onto the beaches of Normandy. The logistic planning for the invasion, a provision for the possible rather than a prediction of the probable, had deemed it conceivable that by now the front line would include the whole of the Cotentin peninsula, be well down towards the Loire and run south from the Orne to Le Mans embracing Falaise and Argentan. Pressure from the politicians for a dramatic breakout was becoming fierce.

Omitted from their considerations was the determination of Hitler not to yield an inch of ground, and his unreasonable directions to hurl the Allies back into the sea – a policy enormously expensive in men and material. Neither could they predict a lucky blow.

RIGHT: 18 July. A Sherman tank roars into action at Cagny. (IWM)

BELOW: The Bourguébus ridge, the wide open country south of Caen; St Aignan from the D80 near Conteville. It was the prospect of using fast tank formations and building airfields that made this area such an attractive objective.

Rommel was constantly on the move, visiting his commanders. On the evening of 17 July he left Vimoutiers to return to headquarters at La Roche-Guyon. Just up the road at the fatefully-named village of Sainte-Foy-de-Montgomery, two RAF Spitfires strafed his car. Rommel was severely wounded, and played no further part in the war.

On the morning of 18 July British tanks ground south from the eastern bridgehead established by the Airborne troops on D-Day. It was scarcely a secret. The commander of 1st SS Panzer, Sepp Dietrich, claimed he had heard them by putting his ear to the ground. In fact, German intelligence had correctly detected the plan and extensive defences were already in place, using a network of resistance points in villages and farms as well as dug-in tanks to act as artillery.

The British advanced along narrow tracks cleared through their own minefields, with the infantry hanging on to the vehicles, heading for Cagny and the railway embankment that lay between them and the open country of the Bourguébus ridge. Then, just north of Cagny they were engaged by 88mm anti-aircraft guns encouraged to recognise these land-bound targets by a German officer wielding a pistol. The British armour sustained terrible losses, and although it attained the heights south of Caen, the desired breakthrough was not achieved. Meanwhile the Canadians cleared the southern part of Caen and the front line stabilised south of the city on 20 July.

The capture of St Lô on 18 July established the American forces on a line from St Lô to Périers and, even more important, shattered the power of the opposing 2nd Parachute Corps. Reinforcements were not available to the Germans; events around Caen demanded much of their strength.

On 24 July the 9th US Air Force dropped 5,000 tons of bombs on a five-mile (8km) front west of St Lô. Bradley had demanded that they fly parallel to the road but the attack went in at right angles. Some 500 Americans were caught when bombs fell short. But the impact on the German front line, manned by the elite Panzer Lehr, was immense. Practically every one of the 40 tanks left to them was damaged or destroyed and, though they managed to get half of those back in service, the steel was going out of the German resistance. As the Americans fought forward through the shattered landscape, they brought into use a 'funny' of their own, the Rhino. The Germans withdrew the bulk of their troops to set up a defensive line further south, leaving small groups of crack troops to hamper the American advance.

But it could not last. The Germans were in disarray, broken into small units and increasingly by-passed and outflanked. Coutances fell on 28 July and retreating German columns were decimated by artillery and air attack. Resistance became a desperate fight to escape the American

advance. German harassment from Vire on the eastern flank did damage but failed to slow COBRA.

On 1 August Bradley handed over command of the US 1st Army to Lt General Courtney Hodges and became the overall commander of the American forces, including the US 3rd Army led by Lt General George S. Patton, Jr. With characteristic disregard for the danger of an exposed flank to the east, Patton had headed with all speed for Avranches, taking the town on 30 July and sweeping on over the bridge at Pontaubault the next day, brushing aside the power of the 77th German Infantry Division. The roads to Brittany, the Loire and the Seine lay open before him and he was not slow to exploit the opportunity.

ABOVE: The Rhino – the American answer to the bocage. Sgt Curtis G. Culin, 102nd Cavalry Reconnaissance, was inspired by a comrade, Roberts, to mount cutting teeth on a tank to smash through the hedges. (TM)

LEFT: 7 July. Patton, sporting his pearl-handled revolver, with a helmeted Bradley and Montgomery in his two-badged beret. (IWM)

FAR LEFT: Operation BLUECOAT. British tanks commence their ponderous advance from Caumont towards Vire, Bény-Bocage and Mont Pinçon, relieving pressure on the Americans to the west. (IWM)

ABOVE: In a clearing close to the chapel amongst the pine-woods on Hill 317 stands the simple, dignified memorial to the men of the 30th US Infantry.

BELOW: Allied domination of the air was a key factor. Typhoons armed with rockets operated from temporary airstrips against German transport and armour. (IWM)

Field Marshal von Kluge, who had taken over command from von Rundstedt and, with Rommel's departure, Army Group B as well, was unable to resist Hitler's demands for an attack to cut through the Americans at the base of the Cotentin peninsula. Given the collapse of the forces opposing Patton and the obviously imminent movement against the Germans by the British and Canadians, the logical move was to withdraw to a new defensive line; the Seine, perhaps. This Hitler would not permit.

On the night of 6 August Allied Intelligence's ULTRA provided the briefest of warnings that a counter-attack was about to hit the Americans south of Vire. Bradley's reaction was to welcome it as an unprecedented opportunity and to leave the troops already in position to handle it while Patton's advance continued.

47th Panzer Corps, a force thrown together with elements of 2nd SS Panzer, the 17th SS and 116th Panzer, newly arrived in Normandy, were launched against Mortain, swiftly overrunning the town and pushing on to within nine miles (14km) of Avranches by noon on 7 August. 700 men of the 30th US Infantry Division were surrounded on Hill 317 which rises steeply to the east of Mortain, crowned with its little chapel and today shrouded in fragrant pine-woods. Called upon to surrender, they persisted in a determined refusal, supplied only by intermittent air drops and even by medical stores fired in by artillery.

By 8 August the German offensive had slowed to a standstill, and the power of Allied aircraft, American Thunderbolts and RAF Typhoons did terrible damage. Inexorably, the Americans pushed the enemy back, leaving a mass of wrecked transport and armour behind them. Hitler redoubled the damage by throwing in 9th Panzer to be decimated here while leaving an open road to the Loire to the south.

On the night of 12 August the US 35th Division relieved their buddies on Hill 317, finding some 300 of them dead or wounded; their endurance a complete answer to doubters of the calibre of the American infantryman.

The momentum of the advance south of this conflict was maintained. On 12 August General Leclerc was in Alençon with his 2nd French Armoured Division, under the command of the American 15th Corps, and the US 5th Division were in Sées. Allied forces had thus reached a point due south of Le Havre and the jaws of the trap were forming for the Germans. The problem for Montgomery was judging the relative progress in north and south; in deciding where the trap should close. He stopped the Americans where they stood to await the Canadians.

Operations TOTALIZE and TRACTABLE

After Operation GOODWOOD the eastern front lay just south of Caen with the Canadians, under General Crerar, holding it. At 11.00 p.m. on 7 August, as the attack on Mortain was at its height, their 400 tanks rolled forward in the wake of a vast bombing raid. Lessons had been learned. Infantry rode on converted self-propelled gun hulls, communications had been improved and searchlights played on the clouds to light their way. They were also encouraged by the knowledge that Panzers had been moved to the American sector for the Mortain attack.

By dawn good progress had been made and the Air Force joined the action. But in the middle of the day, bombs of the USAF fell amongst the advancing troops, and resistance stiffened as the Germans pushed the remnants of 12th Panzer into the action. In the fierce fighting that boiled around the Falaise road the victor of Villers-Bocage, Michael Wittmann, was killed. Action continued into the evening and the following night but the lack of experience of the Canadian and Polish armoured divisions started to tell. On 9 August the 28th, British Columbia, Armoured Regiment was shattered on Hills 140 and 111 near Estrées-la-Campagne. By 10 August the advance petered out – still more than ten miles (16km) short of Falaise.

With the Americans pushing on so swiftly to the south, taking Argentan and halting there on 13 August, progress to form the northern jaw of the trap was vital. Noon on 14 August saw the Canadians and Poles on the move again but the operation had once more been marred by a failure of co-ordination of ground and air; nearly 400 suffered as a result of bombing errors. By the evening of the 15th they were a mile (1.6km) from Falaise, and the main force turned southeast for Trun. The Canadian 2nd Infantry entered Falaise and cleared it of the last resistance by 18 August.

Meanwhile, to the west, German forces were falling back before Dempsey's British 2nd Army. On 16 August von Kluge had finally ordered a retreat, only to be replaced by Field Marshal Walter Model the next day. Von Kluge killed himself on the way back to Germany. Model immediately sought to extract key units from the pocket. The trap was closing.

TOP: To the north of Hill 111 and the memorial to the Canadian 4th Armoured Division the country lies open and peaceful. Here Operation TOTALIZE ground to a halt.

ABOVE: German tank ace Michael Wittmann. (B)

LEFT: Halfway between Caen and Falaise, at Grainville-Langannerie, are the graves of the Polish soldiers who fell in Normandy.

The Falaise Pocket

The River Dives, that same river that formed the eastern flank of floods that drowned some and protected others of the British Airborne forces on D-Day, rises amongst the hills to the east and south of Falaise. Standing above the valley to the south a ridge runs from Argentan, held by the US 80th Infantry Division, on to Bourg-Saint-Leonard, occupied by the US 90th, rising as it goes on east to Exmes, where the French 2nd Armoured Division were established. Turning north, the hills become more formidable, passed only along the ridge or through narrow valleys. As Friday 18 August dawned, these roads to Vimoutiers formed the only exit to the east; the only escape for the 100,000 survivors of the German 7th and 5th Armoured Armies.

An inexorable pressure was being applied by the British from the west, an impenetrable barrier was formed by the Americans and the French in the south, and from the north the Canadians and Poles were closing in, while the Typhoons and Spitfires of the RAF maintained a terrible rain of destruction from above. For the Germans, fuel was in desperately short supply and vehicles were abandoned for

ABOVE: 25 August. The aftermath of retreat; reduced to horse-drawn transport, the German troops were easy targets for Allied aircraft in the Falaise pocket. (IWM)

LEFT: Beyond the quiet orchards rise the rooftops and church tower of Saint-Lambert-sur-Dive. A car approaches the bridge that was the centre of the inferno of August 1944.

RIGHT: The German Tiger tank out-gunned and out-paced anything the Allies could put in the field. This example stands east of Vimoutiers.

horse transport or forced marching. They were faced with the stark alternatives of escape or destruction.

The Canadians and Poles were ordered to establish themselves on the line of the Dives from Trun to Chambois, but the Poles, because of translation problems, found themselves at les Champeaux, nine miles (14.5km) to the north. As 18 August dawned, and having ransacked the headquarters of the 2nd SS Armoured Division, they hastened south, running into the Germans at Coudehard and taking to the heights of Mont-Ormel and Hill 262. They straddled the Chambois-Vimoutiers road and from this eminence they could survey the whole of the Dives basin, but were separated from the Canadians by the little valley that heads up towards Camembert and Vimoutiers – the final escape route.

ABOVE: At St-Lambert, on the Trun road, the endurance of Major D. V. Currie, VC and his men is recorded.

LEFT: At Chambois on 19 August, overlooked by the massive 12th-century keep, Captain Waters of the 359th US Regiment of Infantry and Colonel Zgorzelski of the 10th Polish Dragoons joined hands. They returned on 19 July, 1965 to be made citizens of honour of the town.

LEFT: From the observation platform of the monument at Mont-Ormel the ridge stretches away towards Hill 262. The killing-ground of the Falaise Pocket lies vulnerable below. The last of the Germans to escape passed to the west (the right), along a narrow valley.

By mid-morning on the 18th the 4th Canadian Armoured Division ejected the last of the SS from Trun and closed on Saint-Lambert, where bridges over the Dives remained open. A force under Major D. V. Currie gained Saint-Lambert only by 7.00 p.m. Here Currie was to cling on, harassing the tidal wave of fleeing Germans less than quarter of a mile off. He was awarded the Victoria Cross.

Through the night and into Saturday the tiny pocket seethed with Germans seeking any route to escape, and fighting viciously for survival. The attack from the air and the artillery was continuous. From the heights of Mont-Ormel the Poles exacted retribution for the destruction of their motherland. Soon they found themselves fighting on two fronts as the 2nd SS Panzer, extracted and regrouped at Vimoutiers, attacked from the north-east to keep the gap open. At 7.20 p.m. on the 19th the Poles and the Americans had linked at Chambois. Throughout the night a relentless fire poured upon the retreating troops creeping under Hill 262.

As day broke on Sunday, 20 August, General Meindl and the 2nd Paratroops managed to open a route from Saint-Lambert to Coudehard, the Corridor of Death. The sheer weight of numbers of German troops kept it open and it was hard to distinguish between aggression and flight as they pressed on. All day long the bridges at Saint-Lambert were an inferno of shelling and a tangle of desperate men struggling across the river. The Poles

repulsed attacks and poured fire on the forces still squeezing out of the pocket, though suffering terrible losses themselves. By nightfall only 114 men of the 1,560 that had originally occupied the hill were still fit for action.

In the rain of the Monday morning, the last flurries of firing died away. The Canadians at last made contact with the men on Hill 262. The valley of the Dives was a ruin, strewn with the wreckage of thousands of vehicles and the bodies of thousands of men. The last resistance at Saint-Lambert ceased at noon and a few skirmishes elsewhere flared up and faded as night approached.

While half the German force had managed to escape, most of their equipment had been lost, and 40,000 taken prisoner.

On 25 August the Allies entered Paris.

ABOVE: Languid in the summer heat, the flags of the Allies adorn the memorial to Polish sacrifice at Mont-Ormel.

ABOVE: The battle now far to the east, peace has its price. The suffering of French civilians should never be forgotten. (IWM)

Acknowledgements

Written by Martin Marix Evans.

Photography by Martin Marix Evans. Additional photography by James Davis Travel Photography, Philip Enticknap, David Playne and Jill McNeil.

Archive pictures courtesy of the Imperial War Museum (IWM), the Tank Museum (TM), Robert Capa/Magnum Photos, the Bundesarchiv (B), the D-Day Museum, Portsmouth, and National Archives, Washington DC (NA).

Editorial assistance by Stephen Brooks, D-Day Museum; Graham Holmes, the Tank Museum; Lt Col Terence Otway.

Cartography by The Map Studio, Romsey, Hants.

Designed by Adrian Hodgkins Design, Oxford.

THE LONGEST DAY

On 6 June 1944 the greatest landing-force ever assembled began the Allied liberation of France – and of Europe. For those who survived 'D-Day', and the bloody battles that followed it, the bitter-sweet memories of those momentous hours will never be forgotten; for many others, it was the moment of supreme sacrifice. We now invite you to visit the beaches, landmarks, museums and military cemeteries of Normandy to pay homage to the architects and witnesses of a brilliant achievement.

RAYMOND TRIBOULET, OBE
Président du Comité du Débarquement

PRINCIPAL MUSEUMS IN NORMANDY*

A: **Arromanches.** The Landing Museum.
   Avranches. Museum of the Battle of Normandy.
B: **Bayeux.** Memorial Museum of the Battle of Normandy 1944.
C: **Bénouville.** Museum of the Airborne Forces.
D: **Caen.** Memorial, a Museum for Peace.
E: **Cherbourg.** Fort du Roule, Museum of the Liberation.
F: **Falaise.** Museum of the Battle of the Falaise Pocket.
G: **Merville-Franceville-Plage.** Merville Battery Museum.
   Ouistreham. Atlantic Wall Museum.
H: **Ste-Marie-du-Mont.** Utah Beach Landing Museum.
J: **Ste-Mère-Eglise.** The Airborne Museum.

MILITARY CEMETERIES*

American
1: Colleville-Saint-Laurent
2: Saint James

British
3: Banneville-Sannerville
4: Bayeux
5: Brouay
6: Cambes-en-Plaine
7: Chouain (Jérusalem)
8: Douvres-la-Délivrande
9: Fontenay-le-Pesnil
10: Hermanville-sur-Mer
11: Hottot-les-Bagues
12: Ranville
13: Ryes
14: Saint-Charles-de-Percy
15: Saint-Désir-de-Lisieux
16: Saint-Manvieu
17: Secqueville-en-Bessin
18: Tilly-sur-Seulles

Canadian
19: Bény-sur-Mer-Reviers
20: Bretteville-sur-Laize-Cintheaux

Polish
21: Grainville-Langannerie

German
22: La Cambe
23: Huisnes-sur-Mer
24: Marigny-la-Chapelle
25: Orglandes
15: Saint-Désir-de-Lisieux

MUSEUMS IN ENGLAND

Southsea. D-Day Museum.
Portsmouth. Royal Naval Museum.
Gosport. The Royal Navy Submarine Museum.
Southsea. Royal Marines Museum.
Romsey. Broadlands (the Mountbatten Exhibition).
Weymouth. Nothe Fort.
Bovington Camp, Wareham. The Tank Museum.
London. Imperial War Museum.
Hendon. RAF Museum.
Middle Wallop. Museum of Army Flying.
Aldershot. Airborne Forces Museum.
Southampton. Hall of Aviation.
Chichester. Tangmere Military Aviation Museum.
Dover. The White Cliffs Experience.

* The numbers and letters alongside the names refer to the locations marked on the map, page 1.

COVER MAIN PICTURE: 48th Royal Marine Commando land at St-Aubin-sur-Mer, 6 June 1944. (IWM)

PITKIN

ISBN 0-85372-682-5

9 780853 726821 >